"Any man can be a father, but it takes someone special to be a dad. "

\- Anne Geddes

For Papa
From:

Table of Contents

Introduction

This notebook was made for you—biological and non-biological fathers alike—to record the events that have affected your life.

Future generations will only value our legacy and wisdom if we take the time to share our life stories.

This guided memoir acts as a tool for writing down your ideas, tales, and insights, transforming this guided diary into a treasured gift to pass down to your children, loved ones, and future generations.

The interesting, thought-provoking suggestions make it straightforward to write down everything from childhood recollections and life lessons to future goals.

Once finished, this book will aid your children and future generations in learning more about your family's history.

The most important aspect of this book, though, is that it will chronicle your life. It's what your family will discover about you, and it'll help you form important connections with them. With your experiences, accomplishments, and life lessons, you may influence the next generation and those to come.

How To Use This Book

There are no hard and fast rules for using or finishing this guided notebook. The themes can be tackled in a variety of ways, and the book's format is customizable. You can start at any place and fill in the details in any sequence. You can either jump around and answer questions as you go, or you can start at the beginning and work your way through them in order.

There is no correct or incorrect way to answer any question. You may opt not to respond to some questions, and others may not apply to you at all. In lieu of these questions, feel free to use the additional questions provided on our website.

When answering a question, don't overthink or hold back. Write freely and express whatever comes to mind in the moment. In your responses to all of the questions, try to be as honest, thoughtful, and specific as possible. There's no need to be too formal or concerned about the structure of your answer. Unfiltered and heartfelt comments are the most powerful.

Wherever you can, be specific. Exact details help bring your storey to life. When possible, try to remember as many specific dates, locations, and addresses as possible, as well as brand names and other information. Allow yourself plenty of time to respond to the questions. Because there are so many questions, you may want to spread them out over several sessions, perhaps spending some time each day for a few weeks or months.

You might even enjoy having a family member assist you in setting up a video camera or audio recording equipment and having them ask you the questions out loud before recording your responses. You can use the extra notes pages at the conclusion of each section if you need more room to answer a question. You can also utilise the notes sections to include some memorable photographs.

My Personal Details

Full Name:

Date of Birth:

Place of Birth:

Height:

Eye Color:

Hair Color:

Distinguishing features:

_____

_____

_____

When I Was A Baby

What Year Did I Come Into This World?

_____

_____

On What Date Was It?

_____

_____

Was It A Weekday Or A Weekend?

_____

_____

_____

What Was The Weather Like At The Time Of My Birth?

_____

_____

_____

Where Was I Born?

_____

_____

_____

_____

Is There Anything My Parents Told Me About The Day I Was Born?

_____

_____

_____

_____

_____

_____

_____

What Is My Earliest Memory?

_____

_____

_____

_____

_____

_____

_____

_____

Can I Remember The House Or Apartment
That I Grew Up In?

_____

_____

_____

What Was It Like Inside?

_____

_____

_____

_____

_____

_____

_____

_____

_____

_____

_____

_____

_____

_____

_____

_____

Is It Possible For Me To Describe The Neighbourhood Where I Grew Up?

What Were My Parents Like?

Where Were They From?

_____

_____

_____

_____

_____

_____

_____

What Did They Do To Make A Living?

_____

_____

_____

_____

_____

_____

_____

_____

_____

_____

_____

Did My Parents Have A Favourite Tale About Me When I Was A Baby?

What Was My Parents Marriage Like?

_____

_____

_____

_____

_____

_____

_____

_____

_____

_____

_____

_____

_____

_____

_____

At What Age Were They Wed?

_____

_____

_____

How Many Brothers And Sisters Did I Have?

_____

_____

What Childhood Memories Do I
Have Of Each Of Them?

_____

_____

_____

_____

_____

_____

_____

_____

_____

_____

_____

_____

_____

_____

Did I Have Grandparents Around?

_____

_____

_____

Where Did They Come From?

_____

_____

_____

_____

_____

_____

_____

_____

Do I Have Any Recollection
Of Them?

_____

_____

_____

_____

_____

_____

_____

Are There Any Fond Or Significant Memories I Have Of Them?

Notes

What My Childhood Was Like

What Was I Like As A Child?

_____

_____

_____

_____

_____

_____

_____

_____

_____

_____

_____

_____

_____

_____

_____

_____

My Favourite Food Was

_____

_____

_____

What Did I Like To
Do For Fun?

_____

_____

_____

_____

_____

_____

_____

_____

_____

_____

_____

_____

_____

Did I Have Any Favourite Toys Or Games? What Were They?

_____

_____

_____

_____

_____

_____

_____

_____

My Favourite Item Of Clothing Was

_____

_____

_____

_____

_____

_____

_____

_____

_____

_____

What Obligations Did I Have
Within The Household?

_____

_____

_____

_____

_____

_____

_____

What were some of the vacation destinations
I visited with my family?

_____

_____

_____

_____

_____

_____

_____

_____

_____

_____

My Most Vivid Memory
From A Vacation Is

_____

_____

_____

_____

_____

_____

How Did The Family Celebrate Holidays?
What Traditions Did We Have?

_____

_____

_____

_____

_____

_____

_____

_____

_____

_____

_____

_____

_____

Some Of My Favourite
Pastimes Were

_____

_____

_____

_____

_____

_____

_____

_____

_____

_____

_____

_____

_____

_____

_____

_____

_____

_____

_____

_____

What Was The Best Gift
I Received As A Child?

_____

_____

_____

_____

_____

_____

_____

What School Did I Go To?

_____

_____

_____

_____

_____

_____

_____

_____

I Was A Good/Naughty Student

_____

_____

_____

_____

_____

_____

_____

What Was My Favourite Subject?

_____

_____

_____

_____

_____

_____

Who Was My Favourite Teacher?

_____

_____

_____

_____

_____

_____

What Was One Of My Greatest
Achievements As A Child?

_____

_____

_____

_____

_____

_____

When I Grew Up, I
Wanted To Be

_____

_____

_____

_____

_____

_____

_____

_____

_____

What Did I Get In Trouble For
When I Was Young?

_____

_____

_____

_____

_____

_____

_____

_____

Was There A Time Where I Felt That
I Was Treated Unfairly?

_____

_____

_____

_____

_____

_____

_____

_____

What Significant World Events Do I Recall From My Childhood?

_____

_____

_____

_____

_____

_____

_____

_____

How Does Growing Up Today Differ From When I Was A Child?

_____

_____

_____

_____

_____

_____

_____

_____

Was There A Place Where I Liked To "Hang Out"?

_____

_____

_____

_____

_____

_____

_____

_____

What Kind Of Music Did I Listen To When I Was Young?

_____

_____

_____

_____

_____

_____

_____

_____

Who Was My Closest Childhood Friend?

_____

_____

_____

What Did We Like To Do Together?

_____

_____

_____

_____

_____

_____

_____

_____

_____

_____

_____

_____

_____

_____

_____

_____

Did I Have Any Role Models? Why Did I Look Up To Them?

_____

_____

_____

_____

_____

_____

What Was The Most Important Lesson My Parents Taught Me?

_____

_____

_____

_____

_____

_____

_____

_____

_____

_____

_____

Notes

My Career and Interests

Did I Travel During My Lifetime?

_____

_____

_____

_____

_____

_____

Where Was The Most Interesting
Place I Visited?

_____

_____

_____

_____

_____

_____

_____

_____

_____

_____

_____

Were There Any Creative Endeavours
That I was Involved In?

_____

_____

What Were They And How Did
They Impact My Life?

_____

_____

_____

_____

_____

_____

_____

_____

_____

_____

_____

_____

_____

_____

_____

Am I A Musical Person?

_____

_____

_____

_____

Are There Any Instruments That I Have Been Able To Play?

_____

_____

_____

_____

_____

Are There Any Sports That I Have Enjoyed Playing Or Watching?

_____

_____

_____

_____

_____

_____

_____

_____

My Favourite Author Is

_____

_____

_____

And My favourite Book Is

_____

_____

_____

I Can Speak _ Different Languages

And They Are

_____

_____

_____

_____

My Favourite Pastime Was

_____

_____

_____

_____

_____

_____

_____

What The Most Important Job Role I Ever Held?

_____

_____

_____

_____

At Which Company?

_____

_____

_____

What Was My Favourite Job Role That I Held? Why Was It Enjoyable?

_____

_____

_____

_____

_____

_____

_____

_____

_____

What Are Some Of The Life Lessons I Have Learnt From My Time At Work?

What Were Some Of The Most Important Achievements In My Working Life?

How Have My Dreams And Goals Evolved Over Time?

_____

_____

_____

_____

_____

_____

_____

_____

_____

_____

_____

_____

_____

_____

_____

_____

_____

_____

What Do I Do For Enjoyment Now?

_____

_____

_____

_____

_____

_____

_____

_____

_____

_____

_____

_____

_____

_____

_____

_____

_____

_____

Notes

About My Relationships

What Do I Look For In A Friendship?

_____
_____
_____
_____
_____
_____
_____
_____
_____
_____
_____
_____
_____
_____
_____
_____
_____

What Is/Was My Longest Lasting Friendship And What Was The Secret To Its Longevity?

_____

_____

_____

_____

_____

_____

_____

_____

_____

_____

_____

_____

_____

_____

_____

_____

_____

_____

What Is The Most Important Thing
In A Romantic Relationship?

_____

_____

_____

_____

_____

_____

_____

_____

What Makes A Relationship
Successful?

_____

_____

_____

_____

_____

_____

_____

_____

What Is Different About Romantic Relationships Today Compared To Those In The Past?

In What Ways Am I Similar To And Dissimilar To My Mother?

_____

_____

_____

_____

_____

_____

_____

_____

_____

_____

_____

_____

_____

_____

_____

_____

_____

_____

_____

_____

_____

In What Ways Am I Similar To And Dissimilar To My Father?

Where Did I First Meet My Spouse?

_____

_____

_____

_____

_____

My First Impression Of Her Was

_____

_____

_____

_____

_____

_____

_____

_____

_____

_____

_____

_____

Do/Did My Spouse And I Have Common Interests? What Are/Were They?

_____

_____

_____

_____

_____

_____

_____

Do/Did My Spouse And I Have A Favourite Local Hangout?

_____

_____

_____

_____

_____

_____

_____

_____

_____

_____

What Is The Dearest Memory I Share With My Spouse?

_____

_____

_____

_____

_____

_____

_____

_____

_____

_____

_____

_____

Our Favourite Shared Pastime Is/Was

_____

_____

_____

_____

What Is The Most Romantic Thing That My Spouse Has Ever Done For Me?

What Was Our Most Joyful Day Together? What Happened That Made It So Special?

_____

_____

_____

_____

_____

_____

_____

_____

_____

_____

_____

_____

_____

_____

_____

_____

_____

_____

In What Location Was Our Wedding Held?

_____

_____

_____

What Was Our Wedding Like? Was It A Large Ceremony With Lots Of Friends And Family?

_____

_____

_____

_____

_____

_____

_____

_____

_____

_____

_____

_____

_____

What Is Something That Makes Marriage Challenging?

What Is It That Makes It Worthwhile?

What Would I Tell A Young Person Today That Is Searching For Love?

_____

_____

_____

_____

_____

_____

_____

_____

_____

_____

_____

_____

_____

_____

_____

_____

Notes

Becoming A Father

How Many Children Do I Have?

_____

_____

What Are Their Names?

_____

_____

_____

At What Ages Did I Have My Children?

_____

_____

_____

What Are The Birth Dates
Of My Children?

_____

_____

_____

How Much Did They Weigh At Their
Time Of Births?

_____

_____

_____

_____

Did I Imagine I Would Become A Father At The Age I Did?

_____

_____

_____

_____

How Did I Feel When I First Found Out I Was Going To Be A Father?

_____

_____

_____

_____

_____

_____

_____

_____

_____

_____

_____

_____

_____

How Did Life Change With A Baby Around?

_____

_____

_____

_____

_____

_____

_____

Was It Easy/Difficult To Adapt To Life With A Child in The Household?

_____

_____

_____

_____

_____

_____

_____

_____

_____

_____

What Are The Best Things
About Being A Father?

_____

_____

_____

_____

_____

_____

_____

_____

_____

_____

_____

_____

_____

_____

_____

_____

_____

_____

_____

_____

_____

_____

And The Most Challenging
Aspects Of Fatherhood?

_____

_____

_____

_____

_____

_____

_____

_____

_____

_____

_____

_____

_____

_____

_____

_____

_____

_____

What Have Been Some Of The Biggest Surprises About Fatherhood?

What Advice Would I Give To My Children About Becoming A Parent?

_____

_____

_____

_____

_____

_____

_____

_____

_____

_____

_____

_____

_____

_____

_____

_____

What Is The Advice I Would Give For Dads During The Tough Teenage Years?

What Are The Some Of The Best Memories Involving My Children?

_____

_____

_____

_____

_____

_____

_____

_____

_____

_____

_____

_____

_____

_____

_____

_____

Do I Share Similar Interests
With My Children?

_____

_____

What Are They?

_____

_____

_____

_____

_____

_____

_____

_____

_____

_____

_____

_____

_____

_____

What Are Some Of My Children's Best Traits?

_____

_____

_____

_____

_____

_____

_____

_____

_____

_____

_____

_____

_____

_____

_____

_____

What Was The Most Important Thing In The Home When My Children Were Young?

What Am I Most Proud Of In
My Fatherhood Journey?

_____

_____

_____

_____

_____

_____

_____

_____

_____

_____

_____

_____

_____

_____

_____

_____

_____

Looking Back If I Could Do Anything Differently In Fatherhood, What Would I Do Differently?

_____

_____

_____

_____

What Has Parenting Taught Me About Life?

_____

_____

_____

_____

_____

_____

_____

_____

_____

_____

_____

_____

_____

_____

_____

_____

How Have I Changed As A Person Since Becoming A Father?

_____

_____

_____

_____

_____

_____

_____

_____

_____

_____

_____

_____

_____

_____

_____

_____

_____

Notes

What Life Has Taught Me

What Was The Most Pivotal Moment In My Life?

_____

_____

_____

_____

How Did I Feel About It?

_____

_____

_____

_____

_____

_____

_____

_____

_____

_____

_____

Who In My Life Has Had The Greatest Influence On Me?

_____

_____

How Have I Changed As A Result Of My Experience With This Person?

_____

_____

_____

_____

_____

_____

_____

_____

_____

_____

_____

_____

_____

_____

What Was The Most Frightening
Thing That Ever Happened To Me?

_____

_____

_____

_____

_____

_____

_____

_____

_____

Did It Have Any Lasting Effect On Me?

_____

_____

_____

_____

_____

_____

_____

_____

What Did I Learn From It?

_____

_____

_____

_____

_____

_____

_____

_____

_____

_____

_____

_____

_____

_____

_____

_____

_____

_____

_____

_____

Thinking Back To A Day In My Life That Was Almost perfect. What Happened And What Made It So Special?

_____

_____

_____

_____

_____

_____

_____

_____

_____

_____

_____

_____

_____

_____

_____

_____

_____

Did That Day Influence Me In Some Way?

_____

_____

_____

_____

_____

What Did I Learn From It?

_____

_____

_____

_____

_____

_____

_____

_____

_____

_____

_____

_____

_____

Was I Ever Lost In Life At Any Point?

_____

_____

_____

_____

How Did It Make Me Feel?

_____

_____

_____

_____

_____

_____

_____

_____

_____

_____

_____

_____

How Did I Find My Way
Again Afterwards?

What Have I Enjoyed The Most
About Life So Far?

What Have Been The Most Important Successes In My Life So Far?

_____

_____

_____

_____

_____

_____

_____

_____

_____

_____

_____

_____

_____

_____

_____

_____

Why Were They So Important?

_____

_____

_____

_____

_____

_____

_____

_____

_____

_____

_____

_____

_____

_____

_____

_____

_____

_____

_____

_____

What Piece Of Advice I Received From My Grandparents Or Parents Had The Most Significant Impact On My Life?

_____

_____

_____

_____

_____

_____

_____

_____

Is There Anything I Learned From My Siblings That Has Aided Me In My Life?

_____

_____

_____

_____

_____

_____

_____

_____

_____

_____

What Are Some Things In Life To Avoid Doing?

_____

_____

_____

_____

_____

_____

_____

_____

And Some ThingsTo Make Sure To Do?

_____

_____

_____

_____

_____

_____

_____

_____

What In My Opinion Is The Secret To Happiness?

Notes

My Predictions
For The Future

Do I Think We Will Colonise Other Solar Systems?

_____

_____

_____

_____

Will We Find Life On Other Planets?

_____

_____

_____

_____

Will Commercial Space Travel Ever Be
Affordable For The Average Person?

_____

_____

_____

_____

When Will The U.S Have Its First Female President?

_____

_____

_____

_____

_____

Will People Ever Travel In Flying Cars?

_____

_____

_____

_____

Will Computers Take Over Most Peoples Jobs Eventually?

_____

_____

_____

_____

What Do I Think Humans Would Do To Find Meaning In Their Lives If This Were The Case?

_____

_____

_____

_____

Do I Think Humans Could Ever Stop The Ageing Process And Live Forever?

_____

_____

_____

_____

Do I Think It Would Be Worthwhile To Do That?

_____

_____

_____

_____

_____

Will We Ever Be Able To Control The Weather?

_____

_____

_____

_____

Will We Be Able To Cure Cancer And Heart Disease?

_____

_____

_____

_____

Will We Be Eating Pills And Tablets Instead Of Actual Food?

_____

_____

_____

Will Virtual Worlds Ever Be Indistinguishable From Reality?

_____

_____

_____

_____

Where Do I Think The Future Of Energy Production Lies?

_____

_____

_____

_____

What Could Be The Solution To Fix Climate Change?

_____

_____

_____

_____

_____

Will The Worlds Population Exceed 10 Billion?

_____

_____

_____

_____

Do I Think That We Will Ever Merge With Technology Or Even End Up Living Completely Inside A Digital Realm?

_____

_____

_____

_____

Do I Believe That We Will Be Able To Bring Back Extinct Species?

_____

_____

_____

_____

Will We Develop An Artificial Super Intelligence?

_____

_____

_____

_____

Notes

Messages To My Loved Ones

_____

_____

_____

_____

_____

_____

_____

_____

_____

_____

_____

_____

_____

_____

_____

Notes

Time Capsule

Statistics

Today's date:

City Population:

Country Population:

Country Leader:

World population:

Big event this year:

Prices

Load of Bread:

Book of Stamps:

Average house price:

Average wage:

Mortgage interest rate:

Cup of Coffee:

Petrol/Gas:

Family Tree

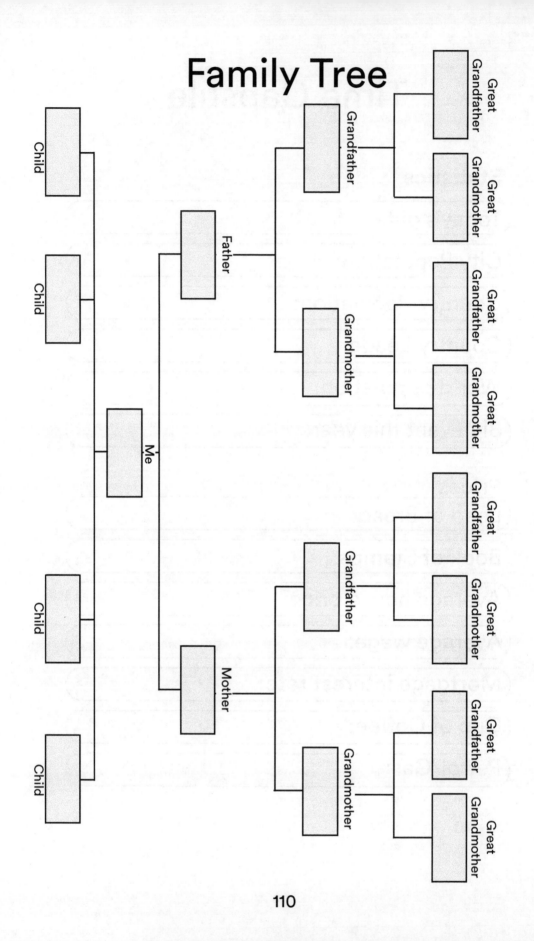

www.ingramcontent.com/pod-product-compliance
Lightning Source LLC
LaVergne TN
LVHW082254110225
803544LV00019B/278